IBD-Friendly Recipes for Crohn's and Colitis

Gut Inspired — Teen Approved

Julie Warshaw and Cara Lanzi

Photography by:

Ken Alswang, At Home Studios

Amanda Warshaw

Design by:

Dedicated Book Services

First Edition
ISBN: 978-0-692-08078-8

This book is dedicated to my daughter, my hero, to my family, and to the many people suffering from this disease, the medical professionals who have devoted their lives to helping patients, and to the dedicated researchers who strive every day to find a cure. Thank you for all that you do.

Dear Readers,

Thank you very much for purchasing this recipe book. As a mom, attorney, and Co-Founder of Cure for IBD, www.cure4ibd.org, I have been involved in raising money to fund promising research to find a cure and to find better, more natural treatments for Inflammatory Bowel Disease (IBD). A portion of the net proceeds from this book will be donated to fund research for a cure.

I have two relatives who suffer from severe Ulcerative Colitis. The day that my daughter was diagnosed with this terrible disease, I vowed to do anything and everything that I could for as long as I could to find a cure. Driven by the devastation that my child was suffering and using my legal skills, I reached out to doctors, researchers, and University faculty all over the world to learn about various treatments and research studies. I got involved in fund raising and connecting with others who shared the same fate. It was comforting, but it was not enough. I needed to do more.

A few generations back, IBD was not as common as it has become today, or perhaps it was just not reported. However, it got me thinking about diet, how food has changed, and whether fast food, packaged and processed foods, pesticides, and microwaves had any effect on digestion. I also wondered about the rampant antibiotics that my children were given every time they had a sinus infection or croup. I started asking questions of the specialists. At first, we were told that diet did not matter and had no effect on IBD symptoms. One doctor said that my daughter should stay away from red meat, but then others said that because she was so anemic, she needed to eat red meat and that it really would not matter. This was quite discouraging.

We read about Gluten-free diets and gave them a try, only to find that for a short time we saw results, but they were not lasting. There were many substitutes used in these mostly packaged foods, such as sugar and additives.

We then found the Seattle Children's Hospital, where Dr. David Suskind and his team were studying the effects of diet and IBD. We went to see his practice and learned about the Specific Carbohydrate Diet (SCD) and about their successes with this diet. We were hopeful that my daughter could also be successful on that diet. I researched everything I could find regarding that diet and we started. Dr. Suskind's team was very helpful with providing resources and connecting us to others on this diet. Unfortunately, she did not like a lot of the foods and she just wanted to be "normal" so the diet was even more challenging. Since this diet is very restricting, eating chicken, soup, and a little bit of vegetables, she became frustrated with the limited options without her plain pasta and bagels, which she subsisted on prior to this diet, her "go to" foods when she was not well. Despite the challenges and not knowing her triggers at that time, she stuck with it. After two weeks, we had testing done and her numbers were significantly better. The only difference had been the diet. That was our moment of hope. She tried to stay on the diet for a few weeks longer but she eventually could not continue. However, with that progress in mind, we would not give up on the notion that diet could affect her disease.

In my research about food, I noticed that within the last 50 years or so, with the rise of processed foods, emulsifiers were added to preserve them longer. I am not a scientist, and although this area is still being studied, I read several articles and research studies that indicated a correlation between the use of certain emulsifiers and the rise in IBD. Getting off packaged goods and processed foods for two weeks and sticking with the most basic foods on the SCD diet brought her test results into a better, almost normal range. I decided to try to find more recipes that she could eat in an attempt to get her back on the SCD diet. We tried another few weeks and again, her numbers went down, indicating that the inflammation was healing. Since it was difficult to stick with the diet or to eat out with friends, I had to find something else that would work.

I then came across the IBD-Aid diet out of the University of Massachusetts. There was a nutritionist, Barbara Olendzki, who gave me so much information and support. We tried the diet but soon discovered that her body could not tolerate many of the foods, as we had yet to fully discover her triggers. However, with the variety of foods allowed on that diet, our hope was restored and my search continued.

It became a matter of degree. The SCD, the IBD-Aid, and probably others are effective healing diets. However, each individual is different and tolerance for various foods differs as well. Finding the balance and what works for your particular situation is the key. Starting a restrictive diet for a small child who grows up only eating certain foods may be easier than for a teenager who has been exposed to a variety of foods, who has food cravings, and who wants to fit in with friends. The severity of a person's disease and individual food sensitivities may also dictate the number of dietary restrictions needed. For us, we needed to find a workable compromise to heal and address the disease, but not let diet take away all of the joy in her life. Again, my search continued.

We began focusing on her triggers, what foods she could eat and what foods made her sick. We noticed that it made a difference when meat, fruit, and vegetables were organic. Whether or not science supports this, we noticed that when she ate meat that had antibiotics, she got very sick. Similarly, if fruit and vegetables had been treated with pesticides, she also got sick. I started buying only organic meat and produce. It was expensive, but I could not take the risk that she would get sicker.

After months of research, I had to adjust the way I cooked and prepared meals. I had always tried to eat relatively healthy foods and to prepare meals that were low in cholesterol and such, but cooking for someone with IBD is very different. Making everything from scratch without any packaged or processed foods and with only organic ingredients and very little variety was a challenge and very time consuming, but I had to try.

After months of trying this on my own, I broke down and hired a professional chef to help me. I researched ingredients that I had never heard of before. At the same time, we tried to determine her triggers. When we discovered her subtle nut sensitivities, it all started to fall into place. By eliminating all nuts and nut flours, we turned to oat flour. After about four years in the making, the result is this book. It contains recipes that worked for my daughter, as well as for others.

The basic "rules" to follow for this diet are the following:

1. **No processed foods of any kind**
2. **Everything that can be organic must be organic, even if the recipes do not specify**
3. **No refined sugar**
4. **No grains**
5. **Use organic oats and organic oat flour**
6. **No dairy**
7. **All vegetables must be cooked well until soft**
8. **Virtually no red meat, only chicken**
9. **Very little fruit and it must be organic**
10. **Sweeteners can only consist of pure organic maple syrup, organic cinnamon, organic pure vanilla, honey, and organic dark chocolate, all used sparingly.**

I know right now you are probably saying there is really nothing left to eat, but I promise you that there is. This diet even appeals to picky teenagers. Since the ingredients are all fresh, many recipes like desserts and muffins can be made in larger batches and frozen for later use. They even defrost well and taste great! Also, it is all a matter of tolerance. Eliminate the foods that you cannot tolerate and add others that you can. If you can tolerate these foods, then look to add other nutritious foods listed in the IBD-Aid diet or similar diets. Creating a healthy, workable diet is really the making of a balanced and sustainable future.

When on this diet, my daughter's test results dramatically improved and the inflammation stayed under control. When she strayed from the diet, her numbers went up and inflammation increased.

These recipes and this homemade diet will not work for everyone, but I truly hope that it inspires others to determine their own individual triggers and sensitivities and what could become sustainable in their life. I will not give up until we find that cure, but for now, we eat smart to fight IBD!

Please note that diet is not the be-all end-all for combating IBD. Medications may be needed as well, but we have been able to avoid using some medications so far because diet has been able to control certain symptoms. I encourage you to find a medical provider who will monitor medications, while at the same time work with you on diet and other healthy alternatives. If you are of school age, I would also encourage you to obtain at least a Section 504 Plan to provide accommodations and protections when you have a flare up or to help prevent stress and a flare up. As an attorney representing children with special needs and medical conditions, I work with many clients whose medical needs are not being addressed at school. It is unfair for someone who suffers from IBD to be expected to turn in homework and assignments and to take tests on time in the midst of stressful and painful flare ups, surgical procedures, blood transfusions, medical treatment, etc. If your school district will not work with you to implement an Individualized Education Program (IEP) or a Section 504 Plan, I would encourage you to reach out to an attorney who specializes in this area of law.

Thank you for taking the time to read this book. I hope that these recipes and our experience will offer hope, encouragement, and some assistance in your fight against this disease. We will not stop until we find a cure!

Julie Warshaw, Esq.
jwarshaw@warshawlawfirm.com

Hello Readers!

Thank you so much for your interest and purchase of this very special recipe book. It is my sincere hope as a professional chef who specializes in health and nutrition that these recipes help to nourish and guide you on your journey of healing and health. As an alum of the Natural Gourmet Institute for Health and Culinary Arts, the leader in health supportive culinary education, I was able to hone my culinary skills and learn how to merge a diverse range of cuisines with health as the common thread. As a practicing private chef, caterer and culinary instructor, my goal is to always help clients achieve optimal health by pairing their dietary needs with culinary preferences. I attract a demographic of people that require special diets so one of the best parts of my job is to create dishes that a client never thought they would be able to enjoy again, without going outside the parameters of their diet.

Upon my first conversations with Julie it became clear that she needed recipes for her family that not only nourished them, but that were easy to prepare and appealed to everyone around her dinner table. Through discussions about preference, ingredients that were tolerable, recipe tests, trial and error, these recipes were born.

Through our many recipe testing sessions, although we are not endorsing these products, we found that the following brands for specific ingredients worked best:

- Arrowhead Mills Organic Oat Flour
- Bob's Red Mill Organic Rolled Oats
- Cold Pressed Olive Oil (any brand) - the practice of cold pressing olives during production helps to retain nutrients in the oil.
- Enjoy Life Brand Dark Chocolate Chips - completely allergen free!
- Califia Almond Milk - I found it has the least amount of additives and preservatives
- Organic Valley Cultured Butter
- San-J Reduced Sodium Organic Tamari OR if allergic to soy, substitute Bragg Liquid Aminos
- Native Forest Organic Coconut Cream
- Watusee Chickpea Crumbs

In these recipes, plain, unsweetened dairy-free yogurt can be substituted for kefir and coconut milk or pea protien milk can be substituted for almond milk.

Through my personal experiences working with clients, family members and friends with IBD, it is my goal to always bring nutritious, but also satisfying and interesting flavors back into their lives. With this book of recipes, I sincerely believe we have achieved just that.

Happy Cooking!
Cara Lanzi
www.simplyhonestkitchen.com

Table of Contents

CHAPTER 4: DINNER

CHAPTER 5: SIDES/SAUCES/DRESSINGS

CHAPTER 6: SOMETHING SWEET

Chapter 1

Breakfast & Grab-n-Go

Berry - Pineapple Smoothie

Serves 2

Ingredients:

1 cup fresh spinach or baby kale, packed
1 cup very ripe pineapple chunks
1/2 cup plain kefir (or plain, unsweetened dairy-free yogurt)
1 teaspoon cinnamon
Pinch ground turmeric
1 teaspoon chia seeds
1/2 inch piece fresh ginger root, peeled
Juice of half a lemon or lime
3/4 cup plain, unsweetened almond milk
2 cups frozen mixed berries
2 to 3 mint leaves

Method:

Add all ingredients in a blender, Vitamix, Ninja or Nutribullet. Blend until smooth and enjoy!

Chunky Monkey Smoothie

Serves 2

Ingredients:

- 1 cup spinach
- 1 frozen banana
- 2 cups unsweetened almond milk
- 1 tablespoon unsweetened peanut butter
- 2 pitted dates
- 3 tablespoons unsweetened cacao powder
- 2 tablespoons chia seeds

Method:

Add all ingredients in a blender, Vitamix, Ninja or Nutribullet. Blend until smooth and enjoy!

Pancakes With Mixed Berry Sauce

Serves 6

Ingredients:

For the Pancakes
3 eggs
1/2 cup unsweetened almond milk
2 tablespoons unsalted organic cultured
  butter
3 tablespoons maple syrup
1 teaspoon vanilla
1 cup oat flour

1/3 cup coconut flour
1 teaspoon baking soda
1/2 teaspoon cream of tartar
1/4 teaspoon salt
1/2 teaspoon cinnamon
Butter to grease pan

For the Berry Sauce:
12 ounces frozen mixed berries
1/2 cup maple sugar
1/2 cup water
Zest of 1 lemon

Method:

1. Grease a non-stick skillet over medium heat.
2. In a medium bowl, whisk together all wet ingredients.
3. In a large bowl, combine all dry ingredients. Combine the wet ingredients with the dry until a smooth batter form.
4. Using a 1/4 cup measure, pour the batter into the prepared pan and gently spread into a 3-5 inch circle.
5. Cook until bubbles start to show on top of the pancake, about 3 minutes. Using a spatula, gently flip and cook another 1-2 minutes.
6. Repeat steps 4 and 5 until all of the batter is used, adding more butter to the pan if the pancakes start to stick.
7. In a small saucepan, combine all of the ingredients for the berry sauce and cook over high heat until the mixture comes to a boil. Reduce the heat to medium low and cook until berries cook down into a syrup and becomes thick, about 30 minutes.

Sweet Potato Breakfast Hash

Serves 4

Ingredients:

3 pounds sweet potatoes, peeled and small diced
1 large yellow onion, small diced
1 yellow pepper, cored, seeded and small diced
1 red pepper, cored, seeded and small diced
3 tablespoons cold pressed extra virgin olive oil
1/2 teaspoon smoked paprika
1/2 teaspoon garlic powder
1/2 teaspoon sea salt

Method:

1. Preheat the oven to 425 degrees. Line 2 baking sheets with parchment paper and set aside.
2. In a large bowl combine all of the ingredients with spoon and mix well.
3. Distribute the potato mixture evenly and in a single layer on both baking sheets, being careful not to crowd the potatoes so they get crispy.
4. Roast for 20 minutes and toss with a spatula or spoon. Continue roasting for an additional 15 minutes until browned and crisp.

Favorite Lemon Muffins

Ingredients:

1 cup coconut flour
1/2 cup potato starch flour
1 teaspoon baking soda
1/4 teaspoon salt
1/3 organic cultured butter or coconut oil, melted
4 eggs (or for vegan, mix 1/4 cup flaxseed meal and 1/2 cup + 2 Tbsp water)
1/3 cup maple syrup
1/3 cup fresh lemon juice (about 5 large lemons)
2 tablespoons water
1 teaspoon vanilla
Zest of 1 lemon

Method:

1. Preheat oven to 375 degrees. Fill a muffin tin with muffin liners and set aside.
2. In a large bowl, whisk together the flours, baking soda and salt.
3. In a medium bowl, whisk together butter or oil, eggs (or flaxseed), maple syrup, lemon juice, water, vanilla and lemon zest.
4. With a wooden spoon or spatula, mix wet ingredients into dry until well combined.
5. Fill the muffin cups about 3/4 of the way until all of the batter is evenly divided into 12 muffin cups.
6. Bake for 25 minutes, checking with a toothpick in the center of the muffin, making sure it comes out clean. Enjoy!

Store in an airtight container in the refrigerator for up to 1 week or freeze for up to 1 month.

Blueberry Cinnamon Muffins with Pecan Swirl

Yield: 8 muffins

Ingredients:

Muffins:
2 large eggs (or for vegan, mix 1/4 cup flaxseed meal and 1/2 cup + 2 Tbsp water)
3 tablespoons fresh lemon juice
1/3 cup organic cultured butter, softened
2 teaspoons vanilla extract
1/3 cup maple syrup
1/2 cup warm water

1 1/2 cups organic oat flour
1/2 cup coconut flour
1 1/2 teaspoons baking soda
1 teaspoon cream of tartar
1/2 teaspoon sea salt
1/2 teaspoon ground cinnamon
1/2 cup fresh blueberries

Topping:
1/3 cup raw pecans
1 tablespoon solid coconut oil
1 tablespoon organic oat flour
1 tablespoon maple syrup

1 teaspoon ground cinnamon
1 large pitted date
pinch sea salt

Method:

1. Preheat the oven to 350 degrees. Line a muffin tin with muffin liners and set aside.
2. Place all of the muffin ingredients except for the blueberries in the work bowl of a food processor and blend until well combined, about 1 minute. Scrape down the sides and blend again until creamy, like cake batter.
3. Pour batter into a bowl and mix in the blueberries.
4. With an ice cream scooper, evenly distribute the batter into the muffin liners, filling each cup 2/3 of the way full.
5. Rinse the work bowl of the food processor and place all of the topping ingredients into it. Pulse a few times until the mixture has the texture of coarse sand. Sprinkle the topping evenly over each muffin and with a toothpick, mix the topping into the muffin batter.
6. Place the muffins in the oven on the center rack and bake for 25 minutes, until a toothpick inserted into the center of a muffin comes out clean. Remove from the oven and let cool. Store in an airtight container in the refrigerator for up to 1 week or freeze for up to 1 month.

Apple Cinnamon Muffins

Yield: 8 muffins

Ingredients:

1/2 cup coconut flour
1/4 teaspoon baking soda
1/4 teaspoon salt
4 eggs (or for vegan, mix 1/4 cup flaxseed meal and 1/2 cup + 2 Tbsp water)
1/3 cup unsweetened almond milk
1/2 cup maple syrup
2 apples, peeled, cored and diced
3 tablespoons cinnamon
2 tablespoons unsalted butter or coconut oil, melted
1/4 cup walnuts, chopped (optional)

Method:

1. Preheat the oven to 350 degrees. Prepare a muffin tin with muffin liners and set aside.
2. In a large bowl, combine the coconut flour, baking soda, salt and cinnamon. Whisk together to combine.
3. In a medium size bowl, combine the eggs, milk, maple syrup, butter or oil. Whisk to combine.
4. Stir the wet ingredients into the dry ingredients. Mix well to combine. Add the diced apple and walnuts.
5. Fill the muffin lined cups about 2/3 of the way with muffin batter. Bake for about 25 minutes, or until a toothpick inserted in the center of the muffins comes out clean. let cool and enjoy.

Store in an airtight container in the refrigerator for up to 1 week or freeze for up to 1 month.

Carrot Muffins

Yield: 8 muffins

Ingredients:

2 cups organic oat flour
1/4 chopped walnuts
1/4 cup raisins
1/2 teaspoon cinnamon
1/2 teaspoon baking soda
1/8 teaspoon salt
3 eggs (or for vegan, mix 1/4 cup flaxseed meal and 1/2 cup + 2 Tbsp water)
1 cup shredded organic carrots
1/4 cup maple syrup
2 tablespoons coconut oil, melted
1 teaspoon apple cider vinegar

Method:

1. Preheat oven to 325 degrees and grease or line muffin tin.
2. Combine oat flour, walnuts, raisins, cinnamon, baking soda, and salt in large bowl. Combine eggs, carrots, maple syrup, coconut oil, and apple cider vinegar in medium bowl. Stir wet ingredients into dry ingredients.
3. Use a large ice cream scoop to fill muffin cups 3/4 full.
4. Bake for 20-25 minutes, until lightly browned and toothpick inserted in center comes out clean.

Store in an airtight container in the refrigerator for up to 1 week or freeze for up to 1 month.

Always Tasty Cinnamon Muffins

Yield: 24 muffins

Ingredients:

2 cups organic oat flour
2 tablespoons cinnamon
Pinch of salt
4 teaspoons baking powder
3/4 cup maple syrup
1 cup plain unsweetened almond milk
6 tablespoons butter, melted
2 eggs
1 teaspoon apple cider vinegar
1/2 cup chopped walnuts (optional)

Method:

1. Preheat oven to 350 degrees.
2. Stir all ingredients. Pour into lined muffin tins.
3. Bake for 14-15 minutes or until a toothpick inserted in the center comes out clean.

Note: Store in an airtight container in the refrigerator for up to 1 week.

Banana Bread

Yield: 1 large loaf or 12 muffins

Ingredients:

1 1/4 cups oat flour
1/4-1/2 cup maple syrup
1/2 teaspoon salt
1 teaspoon baking soda
1 teaspoon apple cider vinegar
Dash of cinnamon
2 eggs
1/2 cup unsweetened butter, melted
3 ripe bananas

Method:

1. Preheat oven to 350 degrees. Stir together the oat flour, maple syrup, salt, baking soda, and cinnamon.
2. Melt the butter and add to the mixture and stir.
3. Add the eggs and apple cider vinegar and stir mixture.
4. Mash the bananas with a fork and then add them to the mixture and mix gently.
5. Pour batter into a greased 8-1/2 x 4-1/2 inch loaf pan and bake for 45 minutes or until a toothpick inserted in the center comes out clean.
6. Alternatively, pour batter into lined muffin tins and bake for 14-15 minutes or until a toothpick inserted in the center comes out clean.

Note: Store in an airtight container in the refrigerator for up to 1 week.

Vanilla Cranberry Power Bars

Yield: 12 bars

Ingredients:

2 cups slivered almonds
1/2 cup sliced almonds
1/4 cup chia seeds
1/4 cup flaxseed meal
2/3 cup dried cranberries
1 teaspoon vanilla
1 tablespoon maple syrup
2-3 tablespoons water as needed

Method:

1. Line an 8x8 inch baking dish with parchment paper and set aside.
2. In the work bowl of a food processor add almonds, chia seeds, flaxseed meal, cranberries, vanilla and maple syrup. Pulse the mixture until well ground.
3. With the motor running, add the water, 1 tablespoon at a time until the mixture begins to come together and resembles a rustic dough.
4. Remove from the food processor and press into the prepared baking dish. Refrigerate at least 1 hour. Once the mixture is cold and firm, it's easier to cut into. Slice into 12 bars and serve.

Oat Bars

Yield: 12 bars

Ingredients:

2 cups rolled oats, coarsely ground in the food processor
1 cup rolled oats
1⁄4 teaspoon sea salt
1⁄4 teaspoon cinnamon

1⁄4 cup maple syrup
1⁄3 cup honey
1⁄4 cup vanilla or plain unsweetened almond milk
1 1⁄2 - 2 tablespoons refined coconut oil

Method:

1. Preheat oven to 350°F.
2. In a large bowl, combine all the dry ingredients. Add the wet ingredients into the dry mixture, stirring until well combined.
3. Transfer the mixture to a lightly oiled 8 x 12 inch baking dish and press it down until evenly distributed. Using a sharp knife, cut to mark out the bars before you bake them to make it easier to fully cut and remove the bars once baked.
4. Bake for 19-21 minutes, then remove and let cool in pan. Once cool, use a sharp knife to fully cut the bars, then remove with a spatula.

"Peanut Butter" Energy Bites

Serves 12

Ingredients:

1/2 cup almond or sunflower seed butter
1/2 cup peanut butter
8 dates, pitted and rough chopped
2 tablespoons flaxseed meal
2 tablespoons chia seeds

1/4 cup maple syrup
2 tablespoons raw cacao powder
1 teaspoon vanilla
1/4 teaspoon salt

Method:

1. Line a small baking sheet with parchment paper and set aside.
2. In the work bowl of a food processor, add all of the ingredients and process until the dates are finely chopped.
3. Remove the blade from the food processor and using a small ice cream scoop, melon baller or tablespoon, scoop the mixture onto the parchment and roll into individual balls.
4. Refrigerate until slightly hardened.

Note: Store in airtight containers for up to 5 days or freeze for up to 3 months.

Our Favorite Granola

Yield: 6-8 cups

Ingredients:

1 1/2 cups raw pecans
1 1/2 cups unsalted, raw sliced/slivered almonds
1 cup raw pumpkin seeds
1 cup raw walnuts
1/2 cup whole salted almonds
1/8 - 1/4 teaspoon ground cinnamon
1/2 cup maple syrup
2 teaspoons vanilla extract
1/2 cup dried cranberries

Method:

1. Preheat oven to 350 degrees. Line a large baking sheet with parchment paper.
2. In a large bowl, combine all of the ingredients except for the dried cranberries, stirring until the nuts and seeds are well coated.
3. Spread the mixture evenly across the prepared baking sheet. Bake for 8-10 minutes and then stir the granola around so that it bakes evenly.
4. Bake for another 10 minutes or until the granola stops feeling sticky to the touch and it becomes like a soft glaze on the nuts and seeds. Do not let the nuts or seeds start to brown.
5. Remove the mixture from the oven and cool completely (about 30 minutes), then break the pieces apart and add in the dried cranberries and mix.
6. You can always adjust the types of nuts and dried fruit to taste.

Note: Store in an airtight container in the refrigerator for 1-2 weeks.

Snackable Oat Cereal

Yield: 12 servings

This simple and tasty cereal is a favorite for breakfast served with fresh strawberries and blueberries or packed in a bag for on-the-go snacking.

Ingredients:

  6 cups organic oats
  1/4-1/3 cup maple syrup
  Dash of ground cinnamon

Method:

1. Preheat oven to 325 degrees.
2. In a large mixing bowl, mix all ingredients together so the oats are lightly coated with maple syrup.
3. Pour mixture on a large baking sheet lined with parchment paper.
4. Bake 8 minutes and then stir mixture so that the oats bake evenly.
5. Bake another 8-10 minutes but do not let the oats brown.
6. Let cool and store in airtight container in refrigerator for up to 1 week.

Chapter 2

Soups

Bone Broth

Serves 8

Ingredients:

2 pounds organic and pasture raised chicken or beef bones

1 onion, large diced

1 leek, green ends discarded and cut into 1 inch pieces

3 carrots, peeled and cut into 1 inch pieces

3 stalks celery, cut into 1 inch pieces

4 cloves garlic

1 tablespoon apple cider vinegar

1 bunch parsley

1 bunch thyme

1 tablespoon sea salt

2 teaspoons ground turmeric

Method:

1. In a large stock pot, place bones, vinegar and 8 cups of water. Set aside while prepping vegetables.
2. Add all other ingredients and bring to a boil over high heat. When it comes to a boil, reduce to a simmer and cook for 6 hours.
3. Every 30 minutes, check the pot and skim off any foam that has floated to the surface.
4. When the broth is done, let cool slightly before straining and transferring to storage containers.

Store in airtight container for up to 5 days or freeze for up to 3 months.

My Sister's Red Lentil Soup

Yield: 10-12 1-cup servings

This soup is so versatile that you can add many more spices if you can tolerate them but either way, this hearty soup is a crowd pleaser and it can be made in larger batches and frozen in airtight containers for up to 1 month.

Ingredients:

2 1/2 cups organic dried red lentils

8-10 cups water

2 28-ounce cans of organic diced tomatoes or use fresh organic tomatoes

1/2 organic sweet onion, small diced

1 tablespoon dried basil

1 1/2 teaspoon salt

1/2 teaspoon pepper

1/4 teaspoon oregano

1 garlic clove, minced or grated (optional)

Method:

1. Rinse the red lentils with water using a strainer and set aside.
2. Fill a large pot with 8 cups of water and add onion.
3. Bring water and onion to a boil and add the red lentils. Turn temperature to simmer.
4. Add the diced tomatoes and spices and stir frequently.
5. Let simmer uncovered for 20-30 minutes until red lentils are soft, adding more water if it gets too thick.
6. Season further to taste.

Cozy Chicken Soup

Serves 8

Ingredients:

2 tablespoons cold pressed extra virgin olive oil

1 1/2 pounds organic boneless, skinless chicken breasts, cut into 1 inch cubes OR 4 cups of leftover rotisserie chicken, shredded

1 onion, large diced

1 leek, green ends discarded and cut into 1 inch pieces

3 carrots, peeled and cut into 1 inch pieces

3 stalks celery, cut into 1 inch pieces

2 Yukon gold potatoes, peeled and small diced

2 parsnips, peeled and cut into 1/4 moons

4 cloves garlic, peeled

1 teaspoon turmeric

8 cups water

2 sprigs thyme

1 bay leaf

1 bunch thyme

1 tablespoon sea salt

1/2 cup chopped parsley

Method:

1. In a large stock pot, heat oil over a medium flame. Add the chicken, vegetables, garlic and turmeric and sauté until the vegetables are slightly softened, about 8 minutes.
2. Add the water, thyme, bay leaf and salt and bring to a boil over high heat. When it comes to a boil, reduce to a simmer and cook for 1 hour.
3. Remove from flame and stir in chopped parsley. Season with more salt to taste.

Store in airtight container for up to 5 days or freeze for up to 3 months.

Roasted Cauliflower Soup

Serves 6

Ingredients:

2 tablespoons extra virgin olive oil

1 medium onion, large diced

1 leek, sliced

1 1/2 teaspoons salt

1 parsnip, peeled and sliced in 1 inch pieces

1 medium head cauliflower (about 2 pounds) cut into 1 inch pieces

1 medium celery root (about 1 pound), peeled and large diced

6 cloves garlic, peeled

6 cups bone, chicken or vegetable broth tamari

Method:

1. In a large pot, heat the olive oil over medium heat. Add the onion, leeks and salt. Sauté until golden, about 5 minutes.
2. Add the parsnip, cauliflower, celery root, garlic and broth. Bring to a boil and cover. Reduce the heat to low and simmer until the vegetables are fork tender, about 20 minutes. Remove from heat and set aside to cool. Add tamari to taste.
3. Once cooled, transfer soup to a blender or Vitamix and puree until smooth and creamy.

Chapter 3

Breads, Chips, Crackers & Snacks

The Most Delish Flatbread

Yields 1 large tray

Ingredients:

1/4 cup cold pressed extra virgin olive oil,
    plus more for brushing the bread
1 teaspoon onion powder
1 teaspoon garlic powder
1-1/4 cups organic oat flour
3/4 cup + 2 tablespoons tapioca starch

1 tablespoon xanthan gum
1 tablespoon + 1 teaspoon double-acting,
    aluminum-free baking powder
1/2 teaspoon kosher salt
1-1/2 cups water

Method:

1. Preheat the oven to 400 degrees. Line a baking sheet with parchment paper.
2. In a large bowl, whisk the onion powder, garlic powder, oat flour, tapioca starch, xanthan gum, baking powder, and salt until well combined.
3. In another bowl, whisk together the water and olive oil. Pour into the dry ingredients, stirring until the batter is well combined.
4. Spoon the dough onto the prepared baking sheet. Using the back of the spoon, spread the dough evenly into a rectangle shape. Depending on how thick you like your flatbread, you can spread the dough from 1/2-3/4 inch in thickness. Brush with olive oil.
5. Place the baking sheet in the oven and bake for 35 minutes, until firm to the touch and lightly golden brown.
6. Let cool in the pan, and then cut into squares or rectangles.

Note: Store in airtight containers for up to 5 days or freeze for up to 3 months.

Add your favorite dried or fresh herbs and spices and pair with any of the dips and spreads in this book!

French-Style Baguette

Yields 1 loaf

This recipe can be slightly more labor intensive but it's so worth it! I urge you to read the directions carefully, and you will end up with a warm, toasty and slightly crumbly baguette that the whole family is sure to enjoy.

Ingredients:

Yeast Mixture:
1/2 cup warm water
1/4 cup cold pressed extra virgin olive oil
2 tablespoons maple syrup

4 egg yolks
1 tablespoon active dry yeast

Egg whites:
4 egg whites

Egg wash:
1 egg white, beaten until frothy

Flours:
1 cup plus 1/3 cup oat flour, divided
1/2 teaspoons salt

4 tablespoons coconut flour, divided

Method:

1. Preheat the oven to 375 degrees. Line a baking sheet with parchment paper a brush with 1 tablespoon olive oil. Set aside.
2. In a large bowl combine the water, oil, maple syrup, egg yolks, and yeast. Whisk together until well combined and set aside.
3. In a separate bowl, add the egg whites. Using a stand or hand mixer, whisk until soft peaks form.
4. In a third bowl add 1 cup of the oat flour with 1/2 teaspoon salt and mix well.
5. Whisk the oat flour mixture into the yeast mixture until well combined.
6. Gently fold the egg whites into the yeast and oat flour mixture, being careful not to press the air out of the egg whites. The more liquid the egg whites become, the flatter the bread will be. The fluffiness of the whipped egg whites will give a light, airy and fluffy bread. This process will take about 15 minutes.
7. Once the egg whites are completely incorporated into the yeast mixture, fold in the coconut flour, 1 tablespoon at a time.
8. Fold in the remaining 1/3 cup oat flour.
9. Carefully transfer the dough from the bowl onto the prepared baking sheet. Using oiled hands, gently form the dough into a baguette shape.
10. Brush the loaf with the egg wash and make a few slashes in the top with a bread knife.
11. Bake for 30 minutes, or until golden brown.
12. Cool, slice and serve.

Baked "Pita" Chips

Serves 4

Ingredients:

1 cup arrowroot powder
1/4 teaspoon baking soda
1/4 cup coconut oil, melted
5 tablespoons cold filtered water
sea salt

Method:

1. Preheat oven to 400 degrees.
2. In a medium bowl combine the arrowroot powder and baking soda. Add the melted coconut oil and mix using a wooden spoon or spatula. Add water and continue to mix until well combined.
3. Using your hands, knead a few times in the bowl, making sure the dough fully comes together.
4. Divide the dough into 2 balls by pressing the dough together. Dough will be very oily.
5. Roll each ball between two sheets of parchment paper until 1/8 inch thick. Carefully peel back the top sheet of parchment and using a pizza cutter or knife, cut into triangles.
6. Repeat step 5 with the remaining dough until all of the dough is shaped into triangles.
7. Sprinkle with sea salt and any other seasonings you like. Bake for 20-25 minutes, until light golden brown.
8. Remove from the oven and allow to cool and gently break apart any pieces that have stuck together. Serve with White Bean Dip, Guacamole, or Hummus!

Store the "pita" chips in an airtight container or bag at room temperature. Freeze after 2 days.

Herb Crackers

Serves 4

Ingredients:

1 cup organic oat flour
3/4 cup tapioca starch
1 teaspoon baking powder
1 tablespoon xanthan gum
3/4 teaspoon sea salt
1 large free range organic egg
2 tablespoons cold pressed extra virgin olive oil
2 tablespoons water
1 tablespoon coconut oil
1 teaspoon thyme
1 teaspoon rosemary
1 teaspoon garlic powder

Method:

1. Preheat the oven to 325 degrees. Line a baking sheet with parchment paper and set aside.
2. In the work bowl of a food processor, add the oat flour, tapioca starch, baking powder, xanthan gum, and salt until blended. Add the egg, olive oil, water, coconut oil and dried herbs, and continue processing until a ball of dough forms.
3. With a rolling pin, carefully roll out the dough between two sheets of parchment paper until it is 1/8 inch in thickness. Carefully peel back the top sheet of parchment.
4. Cut the dough into 1 inch squares using a knife or pizza cutter. Separate the squares and place them on a prepared baking sheet.
5. Bake for 20 to 25 minutes until the bottoms are golden and the edges are slightly browned.

Store the cooled crackers in an airtight container or bag at room temperature. Freeze after 2 days.

Seeded Crackers

Serves 4

Ingredients:

1 tablespoon flaxseed meal
3 tablespoons water
1/3 cup almonds
1/3 cup sunflower seeds

1/3 cup pumpkin seeds
3 tablespoons sesame seeds
1/4 cup olive oil
1/2 teaspoon salt

Method:

1. Preheat the oven to 375 degrees.
2. In a small bowl, add the flaxseed meal and water. Whisk to combine and let rest until the mixture is set, about 15 minutes.
3. In the bowl of a food processor, add the almonds and process to a coarse meal-like texture. Add the sunflower seeds, pumpkin seeds and sesame seeds and pulse a few times, leaving some bigger pieces of the seeds.
4. Transfer the mixture to a medium size bowl and add the flaxseed and oil. With a wooden spoon or spatula, mix very well. The dough will be sticky.
5. Transfer the dough to a large sheet of parchment paper. Place another piece of paper on top of the dough and roll out to 1/4 inch in thickness, using a rolling pin. Peel back the top piece of parchment paper and cut the dough into triangles, squares or rectangles. Carefully transfer the parchment onto a baking sheet and bake for 15 minutes, or until crispy. Let cool and enjoy!

Store the cooled crackers in an airtight container or bag at room temperature. Freeze after 2 days.

Cheddar-Tasting Crackers

Serves 4

Ingredients:

1 cup organic oat flour
3/4 cup tapioca starch
1 teaspoon baking powder
1 tablespoon xanthan gum
3/4 teaspoon sea salt
1 large free range organic egg

2 tablespoons cold pressed extra virgin
  olive oil
2 tablespoons water
1 tablespoon coconut oil
1 tablespoon nutritional yeast

Method:

1. Preheat the oven to 325 degrees. Line a baking sheet with parchment paper and set aside.
2. In the work bowl of a food processor, add the oat flour, tapioca starch, baking powder, xanthan gum, and salt until blended. Add the egg, olive oil, water, coconut oil and nutritional yeast, and continue processing until a dough forms.
3. With a rolling pin, carefully roll out the dough between two sheets of parchment paper until it is paper thin. Carefully peel back the top sheet of parchment.
4. Cut the dough into 1 inch squares using a knife or pizza cutter. Separate the squares and place them on a prepared baking sheet.
5. Bake for 20 to 25 minutes until the bottoms are golden and the edges are slightly browned.

Store the cooled crackers in an airtight container or bag at room temperature. Freeze after 2 days.

Baked Caramelized Onion White Bean Dip

Serves 6

Ingredients:

2 tablespoons cold pressed olive oil
1 yellow or sweet onion, peeled and sliced
1 15-ounce can cannellini beans
1 clove garlic, peeled
Juice of 1 lemon
1/2 bunch parsley, stemmed

1/4 cup cold pressed olive oil
1/2 teaspoon dried oregano
1/2 teaspoon dried basil
1/2 teaspoon salt
Cooking spray

Method:

1. Preheat the oven to 375 degrees. Spray a small glass or stone baking dish with cooking spray and set aside.
2. In a small skillet, heat 2 tablespoons of oil over medium-high heat. Add the sliced onion and sauté until slightly browned, about 5-7 minutes. Lower the flame to medium and cook, stirring every 5 minutes, until onions are a deep caramel color, about 20-25 minutes.
3. Transfer the onions to the work bowl of a food processor. Add the remaining ingredients and process until smooth and creamy. Add salt or lemon juice to taste. Transfer the bean mixture to the prepared baking dish and bake until bubbly, about 15 minutes.
4. Garnish with chopped parsley and serve with pita chips or seeded crackers!

Guacamole

Serves 4

Ingredients:

4 large avocados, halved, pitted and peeled
2 tablespoons lime juice
1/2 teaspoon sea salt
2 scallions, trimmed and thinly sliced
1/2 sweet onion, peeled and small diced
1 cup cherry or grape tomatoes, quartered
1/4 cup chopped cilantro

Method:

1. In a medium bowl, add the avocado, lime juice and sea salt. With a potato masher, mash the avocados until smooth but leaving some small chunks for a delicious texture.
2. Add the scallions, onion, tomatoes and cilantro and fold with a spoon or spatula to combine. Add salt or lime juice to taste. Serve with pita chips or seeded crackers!

Simple Hummus

Yields 1 1/2 cups

Ingredients:

1 tablespoon cold pressed extra virgin olive oil
1 teaspoon ground turmeric
1/2 teaspoon cumin
2 cloves garlic, peeled
1 15-ounce can chickpeas, drained and rinsed
Juice of 1 lemon
2 tablespoons tahini
1/4 teaspoon cold pressed extra virgin olive oil
1/4 teaspoon sea salt, and more to taste

Method:

1. In a small skillet, heat 1 tablespoon of oil over medium heat. Add the turmeric and cumin, stirring with a wooden spoon or spatula until the spices become warmed and fragrant, about 1 minute. Add the 2 whole cloves of garlic to the skillet and cook until slightly browned, about 5 minutes. Keep an eye on the garlic as it cooks, as you do not want it to burn.
2. Transfer the spiced garlic and oil to the work bowl of a food processor. Add the remaining ingredients and process until smooth and creamy. Add salt or lemon juice to taste. Serve with pita chips or seeded crackers!

Salty Baked Pepitas

Yield: 4-6 servings

Ingredients:

2 cups unsalted pepitas (pumpkin seeds)
1/8 teaspoon salt
Dash pepper
Dash garlic powder
1/8-1/4 teaspoon extra virgin olive oil

Method:

1. Preheat oven to 325 degrees.
2. Mix all ingredients and spread on a large baking sheet lined with parchment paper.
3. Bake 6-8 minutes but do not let the pepitas brown.
4. Let cool and serve.

Note: Store in airtight container in refrigerator for up to 1 week.

Chapter 4

Dinner

Spaghetti Squash with Marinara and Ground Turkey

Serves 4

Ingredients:

2 tablespoons cold pressed extra virgin olive oil for brushing
1 large spaghetti squash, about 3-4 pounds
1 pound organic ground turkey
1/4 cup nutritional yeast
1 sweet onion, small diced
2 cloves garlic, minced
1 pound organic ground turkey
1/2 cup fresh basil
1 cup baby spinach, chopped
1 28-ounce can crushed tomatoes
Salt and pepper
1/4 cup chopped parsley for garnish

Method:

1. Preheat the oven to 400 degrees. Fill a deep pyrex dish with 1-2 inches of water and set aside.
2. With a sharp knife, carefully cut the squash in half, lengthwise. Using a spoon, carefully scoop out the seeds from each squash half and place face side down into the prepared pyrex dish. Place the squash in the oven for 30 minutes, until soft.
3. Remove from the oven and with a spatula carefully flip so that the face of the squash is facing up. Using a fork, scrape the flesh of the squash to create a spaghetti-like texture. Leave the spaghetti in the squash and set aside.
4. In a large sauté pan, heat the olive oil over medium-high. Add the diced onions and cook until translucent, about 10 minutes. Add the garlic, nutritional yeast, and ground turkey, breaking up the meat into small crumbles using a wooden spoon. Season with salt and pepper and cook until the meat is cooked through.
5. Add the crushed tomatoes, basil and spinach and bring to a simmer. Simmer for about 10 minutes, until all of the flavors are well blended.
6. Evenly distribute the turkey-sauce mixture between the squash halves. Place in the oven for 10 minutes, until squash and turkey are slightly browned and sauce is bubbly.
7. Garnish with parsley and enjoy!

Homemade Marinara Sauce
with Acorn Squash

Yield: 6 servings

This sauce can be served with zucchini, butternut squash, or kale pasta.

Ingredients:

8 organic large tomatoes, small diced
1-2 cloves garlic (optional)
1/3-1/2 sweet onion, finely chopped
1 teaspoon salt
1/4 teaspoon pepper
6-8 fresh basil leaves or 1 tablespoon dried basil
2 1/2 tablespoons extra light virgin olive oil

Method:

1. Cook zucchini, butternut squash, or kale pasta, drain and set aside.
2. Sauté the tomatoes, garlic, onion, salt, pepper and olive oil on medium-low heat until tomatoes start to soften.
3. Add basil and cook until tomatoes are wilted and soft.
4. Serve over pasta or if you prefer, puree the tomato mixture in a blender or food processor and then serve over pasta. Salt and pepper to taste.

Note: Try this marinara over delicious, seasonal roasted acorn squash. Preheat oven to 375 degrees. Cut the squash in half and scoop out the seeds with a spoon. Place the two squash halves on a baking sheet and drizzle with a little olive oil. Sprinkle with salt and pepper and bake for 45 minutes to 1 hour. Spoon the fresh marinara over top and enjoy!

Fresh Oat Flour & Kale Pasta

Serves 4

Ingredients:

1/2 bunch organic kale, stemmed, washed and dried
2 cups oat flour
1 1/2 teaspoons salt
2 eggs
2 tablespoons extra virgin olive oil
2-4 tablespoons water

Method:

1. In the work bowl of a food processor, add the kale and pulse until finely minced.
2. Add the oat flour and salt and pulse to combine with kale. Add the eggs, one at a time while blending with kale, salt, and oat flour.
3. With the food processor motor running, add oil. Add 1 tablespoon of water at a time, incorporating with flour.
4. Oat flour becomes moist fairly quickly. Work dough with the heel of the hand for 3-5 minutes. Cover with inverted bowl and let rest.
5. Cut dough into quarters and flatten with hands and press pasta through a pasta machine. Cut pasta to preferred lengths (usually 8-10 inches). Let rest on a towel for up to an hour.
6. Bring lightly salted water to a rolling boil in a 2 quart pan on the stove. Add pasta and cook for 2 minutes, careful not to stir the pasta as breakage may occur. Drain and serve.

Butternut Squash/Zucchini Squash Noodles

Serves 4

Ingredients:

1-2 medium butternut squash (2-1/4–2-1/2 pounds total), peeled, halved and seeded
OR 5-6 medium zucchini (2-1/4–2-1/2 pounds total), ends trimmed
3/4 teaspoon salt
1 tablespoon extra virgin olive oil

Method:

1. Using a spiral vegetable slicer place the trimmed butternut squash/zucchini on the spike of the spiralizer and turn the handle to run it through the blades. Repeat until all of the butternut squash/zucchini has been made into noodles.
2. Place the noodles in a colander and toss with salt. Let drain for 15 to 30 minutes, then gently squeeze to remove any excess water. Add 1 tablespoon of oil to the pan.
3. Add the drained noodles and gently toss until hot, about 3 minutes. Transfer to the bowl, add your favorite sauce and gently toss to combine.

Notes for Using Spiralizer:

- Vegetable should be 2 inches or larger in diameter for smooth continuous noodles. Anything smaller will result in half-moon shaped noodles or sliced veggies.
- Cut both ends off completely straight so that the vegetable can lay flush with the spiralizer (for better grip).

Crispy Cauliflower Pizza Crust

Yields 1 10″ pizza crust

Ingredients:

- 1 medium head cauliflower (about 2 pounds), trimmed and broken into small florets
- 1 tablespoon plus 1 teaspoon extra virgin olive oil, divided

- 1/4 teaspoon salt
- 1 large egg, lightly beaten
- 1/2 teaspoon dried basil
- 1/2 teaspoon dried oregano
- 1/2 teaspoon garlic powder

Method:

1. Preheat oven to 450 degrees. Line a pizza pan or rimless baking sheet with parchment paper. Place cauliflower in a food processor and pulse until reduced to rice-size crumbles.
2. Transfer to a large nonstick skillet and add 1 tablespoon oil and salt. Heat over medium-high, stirring frequently, until the cauliflower begins to soften slightly (but do not let it brown), 8 to 10 minutes. Transfer to a large bowl to cool for at least 10 minutes.
3. Add egg, basil, oregano and garlic powder to the cooled cauliflower; stir to combine.
4. Spread the mixture onto the prepared baking sheet, shaping into an even 10-inch round.
5. Drizzle the remaining 1 teaspoon olive oil over the top.
6. Bake the pizza until the top begins to brown, 10 to 14 minutes.
7. Top with your favorite sauce and pizza toppings and bake until nicely browned all over, 8 to 14 minutes more. Cut into slices and serve.

Pumpkin Pizza Crust

Yields 1 9″ pizza crust

Ingredients:

- 1/2 cup coconut cream
- 2 tablespoons organic pumpkin puree
- 3 tablespoons cold pressed extra virgin olive oil, divided
- 1 1/2 teaspoons maple syrup
- 2/3 cup organic oat flour
- 1/4 cup coconut flour

- 1/2 teaspoon garlic powder
- 1/2 teaspoon dried basil
- 1/2 teaspoon dried oregano
- 1/2 teaspoon dried rosemary
- 1/2 teaspoon salt
- 1/4 teaspoon baking soda

Method:

1. Preheat oven to 425 degrees. Line a baking sheet with parchment paper and brush with 1 tablespoon of olive oil and set aside.
2. In a large bowl, whisk together the coconut cream, pumpkin puree, remaining 2 tablespoons of olive oil, and maple syrup.
3. Stir in the flours, spices, salt, and baking soda. With a spoon or spatula, gently mix until a dough forms. Using your hands, form into a ball.
4. Transfer the dough to the prepared baking sheet. Using your hands, press the dough into a thin circle, about 1/4 inch thick.
5. Place in the oven and bake for 20 minutes. Carefully flip the crust and top with desired sauce and toppings.
6. Bake for 10 minutes until crisp. Slice and serve!

Crispy Chicken Tenders
with Chickpea Breadcrumbs

Yields 8-10 tenders

All I have to say about these chicken tenders is, WOW. With the introduction of chickpea crumbs to the market, it has been a game changer in cooking with recipes that call for conventional breadcrumbs. Aside from the chickpea crumbs, the breading has oat flour for extra coating and iron, as well as spices for flavor. I recommend making these in a double batch because they will not last long once they hit your dinner table!

Ingredients:

1 cup refined coconut oil, plus more for frying as needed
1 pound chicken breast tenders
1 egg, beaten
1 cup chickpea breadcrumbs
1 cup oat flour
1 teaspoon garlic powder
1/2 teaspoon salt

Method:

1. In a 9-inch cast iron skillet, heat the oil over medium-high.
2. In a large bowl, add the chickpea bread crumbs, oat flour, garlic powder and salt. Mix well to combine.
3. Dip chicken pieces into egg, then dredge in crumb mixture. To help the coating stick, set the chicken aside to rest for about 5 minutes.
4. Check your oil temperature with a candy thermometer if necessary (you should be around 375 degrees) or drop in a little bit of flour. If it sizzles immediately, the oil is ready for frying. Add about 5 pieces at a time and cook until golden brown on each side, about 8 to 10 minutes. Turn, and repeat until all brown. Cook the rest of the chicken in batches. Transfer to a paper towel lined plate and sprinkle with a little more salt if needed.

Note: Store in airtight containers for up to 5 days or freeze for up to 3 months.

Chicken Meatballs with BBQ Sauce

Yield: 4 servings

Ingredients:

For the Meatballs:
1 pound ground chicken
1/4 cup unsweetened, original almond milk
1/4 cup cilantro, chopped
1/4 cup red onion, chopped
1/2 teaspoon salt
1 tablespoon extra virgin olive oil

For the BBQ Sauce:
2 tablespoons refined coconut oil
1 large yellow onion, roughly chopped
6 cloves garlic, chopped
3 cups pitted cherries, fresh or frozen
1/4 cup maple syrup
1/4 cup apple cider vinegar
1 teaspoon smoked sea salt

Method:

1. Preheat the oven to 375 degrees. Line a baking sheet with parchment paper and grease with the olive oil.
2. Combine the chicken, almond milk, cilantro, and red onion and salt and form into 1-inch balls. Place on the prepared baking sheet and bake for 30 minutes, until meatballs are cooked through.
3. To make the BBQ sauce, heat the coconut oil in a saucepan on medium heat. Add the onion, and cook for 7-10 minutes or until browned. Add the garlic and cook for another couple of minutes, stirring, until fragrant.
4. Add the cherries, maple syrup, cider vinegar and smoked sea salt. Cook uncovered for 20 minutes, or until the mixture thickens considerably.
5. Transfer to a blender and blend on high until thoroughly mixed.
6. Serve meatballs with BBQ sauce drizzled on top or on the side as a dipping sauce.

Lemon-Oregano Chicken

Serves 6

Ingredients:

2 pounds boneless, skinless chicken breasts cut into 1 inch pieces
1/4 cup fresh lemon juice
2 teaspoons red wine vinegar
3 cloves garlic, minced
1 tablespoon dried oregano
1 teaspoon dried basil
1/2 teaspoon maple syrup
1/2 teaspoon Dijon mustard
pinch of sea salt
1/2 cup cold pressed extra virgin olive oil
Canola oil to grease pan

Method:

1. In a large bowl, whisk together the lemon juice, vinegar, garlic, oregano, basil, maple syrup, Dijon mustard, and salt. Slowly drizzle in the olive oil while whisking continuously until all the marinade ingredients are well combined.
2. Marinate the chicken for at least 1 hour in the fridge.
3. Preheat a grill pan or cast iron skillet to medium-high heat. Grease the pan with canola oil and working in batches, add the chicken and cook until all sides of chicken are browned and the center is cooked through. Serve over greens or as a main dish with cauliflower rice and a side of veggies!

Mom's Baked Chicken

Yield: 4-6 servings

Ingredients:

4-6 thinly sliced organic chicken breasts
1 teaspoon salt
1/4 teaspoon pepper
1/4 teaspoon rosemary
Dash of garlic powder
Dash of oregano
2-3 tablespoons extra light virgin olive oil

Method:

1. Preheat oven to 425 degrees.
2. Wash and place chicken slices in baking pan.
3. Mix spices and olive oil and spread over chicken.
4. Cover loosely with aluminum foil.
5. Bake until cooked through, about 15 minutes.

Chicken and Spinach Burgers

Yields 8 burgers

Flavorful, nutrient dense, and a crowd pleaser for an easy weeknight dinner or a weekend cookout!

Ingredients:

    2 teaspoons refined coconut oil or canola oil
    2 pounds ground chicken or turkey
    1/2 cup red onion, finely diced
    2 cups baby spinach finely chopped
    1/2 teaspoon salt
    1 teaspoon garlic powder
    1 teaspoon onion powder
    1 teaspoon turmeric
    1 1/2 teaspoon dried oregano

Method:

1. Preheat oil over medium heat in a large cast iron skillet.
2. Mix ground chicken or turkey, red onion, spinach, and seasonings in a large bowl until well combined. Divide into 8 equal portions and form burger patties.
3. Cook burgers for 7-8 minutes per side or until they reach an internal temperature of 165 degrees.
4. Serve warm over roasted vegetables, a bed of spinach, or in a lettuce wrap.

Note: Store in an airtight container for up to 5 days or freeze for up to 3 months.

Power Veggie Burgers

Yields 8 burgers

Ingredients:

2 pounds sweet potatoes (white or yellow flesh), washed and skins scrubbed
3 tablespoons reduced-sodium tamari
1⁄4 cup Worcestershire sauce
1⁄4 yellow onion, roughly chopped
1 can cannellini beans, rinsed and drained
1 1⁄4 cups organic gluten-free rolled oats
3⁄4 cup raw walnuts, crushed
1⁄4 cup chia seeds
3⁄4 cup flaxseed meal
1/4 cup chopped parsley

Method:

1. Preheat the oven to 400 degrees. Line a baking sheet with parchment paper, place the whole sweet potatoes onto the tray, and bake for 40 minutes to 1 hour, or until fork tender. Remove from the oven and let cool.
2. Once cooled, peel skins off of the potatoes and add the potato flesh in a food processor. Add tamari, Worcestershire sauce, onion and cannellini beans and pulse until fully combined, stopping the food processor and using a spatula or wooden spoon to move the mixture around. Mix just until the cannellini beans and onion are fully incorporated.
3. In a large bowl, whisk together the oats, walnuts, chia seeds, flaxseed meal, and parsley. Scoop the sweet potato mixture from the food processor and fold into the dry ingredients. Measure out 1/2 cup of the mixture at a time placing on prepared baking sheet, and using your hands, press into round burger-shaped patties. Place the baking sheet into the oven and bake in preheated oven for 15 minutes on each side.
4. Serve with your favorite toppings and sauces!

Note: Store in an airtight container for up to 5 days or freeze for up to 3 months.

Vegan Chickpea Burgers

Vegans, vegetarians and carnivores alike will love these burgers because not only are they packed with flavor but they have a crispy texture.

Ingredients:

Coconut or olive oil spray for the baking sheet
1 15-ounce can organic chickpeas, rinsed and drained
1/2 cup red onion, small diced
1 cup organic gluten-free rolled oats
1/2 cup raw walnuts
1/2 teaspoon garlic powder
1/2 teaspoon onion powder
1/2 teaspoon oregano
1/2 teaspoon dried rosemary
2 tablespoons flaxseed meal
3 tablespoons tamari
1/2 cup fresh parsley, chopped

Method:

1. Preheat the oven to 400 degrees. Line a large baking sheet with parchment paper, spray with cooking spray and set aside.
2. In the work bowl of a food processor, add the chickpeas, red onion, rolled oats, walnuts, spices, flaxseed meal, tamari and parsley. Pulse until completely combined, about 1 minute.
3. With a 1/3 cup measure, portion out the burger mixture onto the parchment lined baking sheet. Form into burger-shaped patties and bake for 20 minutes on the middle rack of the oven.
4. Carefully flip the burgers with a spatula and bake for 10 minutes more. Remove the patties from the oven, cool and serve.

Note: Store in an airtight container for up to 5 days or freeze for up to 3 months.

Crust-Free Spinach Quiche

Yield: 1 9-inch quiche

Ingredients:

1 8-ounce package frozen organic chopped spinach
5-6 slices of organic dairy-free Swiss cheese or dairy free cheddar cheese
3 eggs
1/3 organic onion, small diced
1 teaspoon dried basil
1/2 teaspoon salt
1/4 teaspoon pepper
Cooking spray or butter to grease pan

Method:

1. Preheat oven to 350 degrees.
2. Defrost spinach in microwave for 4-6 minutes in a vegetable steamer.
3. Squeeze out excess water with paper towels.
4. Cut cheese into small pieces, about 1/2-inch long.
5. Add all ingredients to a mixing bowl and stir.
6. Pour mixture into a greased pie pan and bake for 15-20 minutes until the top is golden brown.

Chapter 5

Sides/Sauces/Dressings

String Bean & Mushroom Bake
with Frizzled Shallots

Serves 6

Ingredients:

Gravy:
1 1/2 cups raw cashews, soaked for 4 hours
2 1/2 - 3 cups chicken, beef or vegetable broth
2 tablespoons extra virgin olive oil
1 medium onion, medium diced
4-5 large garlic cloves, peeled and sliced
1/2 cup (or more) organic dry white wine
1 tablespoon lemon juice
1 1/2 teaspoons fresh thyme or 3/4 teaspoon dried thyme
1 tsp sea salt

String Bean Bake:
2 pounds string beans, trimmed
16 ounces cremini mushrooms, stemmed and thin sliced
1/2 cup + 2 tablespoons extra virgin olive oil
10 shallots, peeled and sliced into 1/2 inch rings

Method:

For the Gravy:
1. Drain the soaked cashews and transfer to food processor. Set aside.
2. In a large sauté pan, heat the olive oil over medium-high. Add the onion and garlic and cook until lightly browned, about 7 minutes, stirring as needed.
3. Transfer the onion/garlic mixture to food processor with the cashews. Set the pan aside for later use. Add 2 cups of broth to the food processor and blend until smooth, about 3 minutes.
4. Pour the cashew mixture back into the pan that you cooked the onions and garlic in. Add the thyme and cook the cashew mixture over a medium heat until it thickens and darkens up a little bit, about 2 minutes. Whisk constantly so that it doesn't burn.
5. Whisk in the wine, lemon juice and salt. Continue stirring as it thickens, about 2 minutes. Add the leftover broth to reach desired thickness.

Note: Gravy can be made a day ahead of time, cooled and stored in an airtight container. Reheat over a low or medium-low heat, stirring constantly until warm. Gravy is very thick when cold but thins out nicely when heated.

For the String Bean Bake:
1. Heat the 1/2 cup of oil in a small sauté pan over medium heat until it starts to shimmer. Reduce the heat to low, then add the shallots and cook for 30 minutes or until they reach a golden-brown color. Stir occasionally to ensure even browning. Using a slotted spoon, remove shallots from the oil, drain well and let cool on paper towels.
2. Preheat oven to 400 degrees.
3. Bring a large pot of water to a boil. Blanch the green beans in boiling water for 1 minute then drain.
4. Heat a large sauté pan or Dutch oven over medium-high heat, add 2 tablespoons of oil and cook the mushrooms until soft. In a large bowl, combine the mushrooms, green beans and gravy and mix until evenly coated.
5. Transfer the mixture to a casserole dish and top with crispy shallots. Bake 20 minutes or until the gravy begins to bubble and serve.

Note: Store in an airtight container for up to 5 days or freeze for up to 3 months.

Steel Cut Bruschetta Oat Pilaf

Yield: 4 servings

Ingredients:

2 cups organic steel cut oats
3 1/2 cups water
1/4 teaspoon plus 1/8 teaspoon salt
2 large organic tomatoes, small diced
1/4 sweet onion, finely chopped
1/2 teaspoon dried basil
2-3 tablespoons extra virgin olive oil

Method:

1. In a large pot, add water and 1/4 teaspoon salt and let it come to a brief boil.
2. Lower the temperature to simmer and add steel cut oats.
3. Cook until they are soft and similar consistency to a rice pilaf.
4. In the meantime in a separate bowl, add the tomatoes, onion, basil, 1/8 teaspoon salt, and olive oil and mix into a bruschetta.
5. Add the bruschetta mixture to the steel cut oats and serve as a side dish.

Note: The steel cut oats can be used to substitute for rice pilaf and can be served plain, with stir fried vegetables, or add tofu and spinach if tolerated for added nutrients.

Roasted White Sweet Potato Salad with Pesto

Serves 6

Ingredients:

For the Potato Salad:
5-6 cups white sweet potato, cubed (about 3 pounds)
2 teaspoons cold pressed extra virgin olive oil
1/4 teaspoon sea salt
1/3 cup red onion, finely diced

For the Pesto:
2 cups fresh basil, packed
2 garlic cloves, crushed
1/4 teaspoon coarse sea salt
1 teaspoon lemon juice
1/4 cup cold pressed extra virgin olive oil

Method:

1. Preheat oven to 425 degrees. Line a large baking sheet with parchment paper.
2. Toss the sweet potatoes with olive oil and spread on the baking sheet. Sprinkle with sea salt.
3. Bake for 15 minutes. Toss and continue to cook for another 10 minutes, until just tender.
4. To make the pesto, combine all ingredients in a food processor and process until smooth.
5. Remove potatoes from the oven and allow to cool. Transfer to a serving dish and toss with red onion and pesto sauce.

Cauliflower Rice

Yields 3 cups

Ingredients:

1 large head cauliflower
1 tablespoon extra virgin olive oil

Method:

1. Wash and thoroughly dry cauliflower. Remove all greens, stem and cut into quarters.
2. In a food processor with the grater attachment, grate the cauliflower into the size of rice, leaving any large, tough stems behind.
3. Transfer to a clean towel or paper towel and press to remove any excess moisture.
4. In a large pan, add the oil and cauliflower and sauté the over medium heat. Cover with a lid so the cauliflower steams and becomes more tender. Cook for a total of 5-8 minutes, then season to taste.

Root Vegetable Mash

Serves 6

Ingredients:

1 pound parsnips, peeled and cubed
1/2 pound turnips, peeled and cubed
1/2 cup chicken, bone or vegetable broth
3 tablespoons extra virgin olive oil
1/2 teaspoon salt
1/4 teaspoon dried thyme
pinch of pepper

Method:

1. Fill a pot with cold water and add the parsnips and turnips. Bring to a boil, then partially cover and cook for 15 minutes, until fork tender.
2. Drain the vegetables then transfer to a large bowl.
3. Add the broth, oil, salt and thyme. With a potato masher, mash the vegetables together until desired consistency is reached.

Vegetable Stir Fry

Yield: 6-8 servings

The nice thing about this stir fry is that it can be made with just about any vegetables that you like and can tolerate.

Ingredients:

- 1 bunch broccoli, large diced
- 1 head of cauliflower, large diced
- 2-3 cups of baby carrots, large diced
- 3 cups brussel sprouts, cut in halves
- 1/2 sweet onion, small diced
- 12 asparagus stalks
- 2 cups cut string beans
- 1 red pepper
- 1 green pepper
- 1 yellow pepper
- 1 orange pepper
- 1 tablespoon dried basil
- 1 teaspoon salt
- 1/2 teaspoon pepper
- 1/4 teaspoon garlic powder or 1 fresh garlic clove
- 1/3 cup extra virgin olive oil

Method:

1. Cut all vegetables and add to a large frying pan.
2. Add spices and olive oil and cook on medium heat until the vegetables are soft.
3. Add additional olive oil if needed. Season further to taste.

Spinach-Basil Pesto

Serves 4

Ingredients:

2 cups baby spinach, packed
2 cups fresh basil, packed
2 garlic cloves, crushed
1/4 teaspoon coarse sea salt
1 teaspoon lemon juice
1/2 cup cold pressed extra virgin olive oil

Method:

- Combine all of the ingredients in a food processor and process until smooth.

Avocado-Basil Pesto

Serves 4

Ingredients:

1 ripe avocado, halved and pitted
1 cup packed fresh basil leaves
1/4 cup unsalted shelled pistachios
2 tablespoons lemon juice
1/4 cup extra virgin olive oil
3 cloves garlic, minced
1/4 teaspoon salt
pepper to taste

Method:

- Combine avocado, basil, pistachios, lemon juice and 1/4 teaspoon salt in a food processor. Pulse until finely chopped. Add 1/4 cup olive oil and process until smooth. Add pepper to taste.

Creamy Balsamic Vinaigrette

Yield: 3/4 cup

Ingredients:

1/4 cup balsamic vinegar
1 tablespoon tamari
1 1/2 tablespoons Dijon mustard
1 1/2 tablespoons maple syrup
3 tablespoons kefir (or plain, unsweetened dairy-free yogurt)
1 tablespoon extra virgin olive oil

Method:

1. In glass bowl, whisk together all ingredients until smooth.
2. Store in a jar or airtight container for up to 1 week until ready to serve.

Simple Vinaigrette

Yield: 1 cup

Ingredients:

1/2 cup olive oil
1 tablespoon (1/2 ounce) finely chopped shallots
3 tablespoons red wine vinegar
2 tablespoons maple syrup
1/2 teaspoon Dijon mustard

Method:

1. Combine all ingredients in a blender and blend until smooth.
2. Store in a jar or airtight container for up to 1 week until ready to serve.

Ranch Dressing

Yield: 1 cup

Ingredients:

1/2 cup avocado oil or extra light olive oil
1/2 cup full-fat unsweetened coconut milk, blended if separated
1 tablespoon red wine vinegar
1/2 teaspoon sea salt
1/2 teaspoon black pepper
1/2 teaspoon onion powder
1/2 teaspoon granulated garlic
1 teaspoon dried parsley
1 teaspoon dried cilantro
1 teaspoon dried dill

Method:

1. Place all ingredients in a blender and blend until smooth. Place in the refrigerator overnight to thicken.
2. Store in a jar or airtight container for up to 1 week until ready to serve.

Chapter 6

Something Sweet

Chocolate Chip Scones

Yields 8 scones

Ingredients:

1 1/2 cups organic oat flour
1/2 cup potato starch
1/2 teaspoon baking soda
1/2 teaspoon kosher salt
1/2 cup or 1 stick chilled organic cultured butter, cut into 1 inch cubes
1/2 cup maple syrup
2 large eggs
3/4 teaspoon apple cider vinegar
1 cup dark chocolate chips (Enjoy Life brand - dairy, nut & soy free)

Method:

1. Preheat the oven to 350 degrees. Line a baking sheet with parchment paper and set aside.
2. In the work bowl of a food processor, add the oat flour, potato starch, baking soda and salt and process until combined.
3. Transfer the flour mixture to a large bowl and add the cold butter cubes. With a pastry cutter or fork, work the butter into the flour until the texture of the flour resembles a coarse sand and the butter is about the size of a pea.
4. In a small bowl, whisk the eggs. Whisk in the maple syrup and vinegar. Pour into the flour mixture and mix briefly, just until the dough comes together. Do not over mix.
5. Fold in the chocolate chips.
6. With an ice cream scooper or 1/4 cup measuring cup, scoop the dough onto baking sheet with 2 inches between each scone.
7. Bake for 35-40 minutes or until firm and golden. Cool for 15 minutes, cut and serve.

Note: Store in an airtight container for up to 5 days or freeze for up to 3 months.

Cinnamon Scones

Yields: 8 scones

Ingredients:

1 1/2 cups organic oat flour
1/2 cup potato starch
1/2 teaspoon baking soda
1/2 teaspoon kosher salt
2 teaspoons cinnamon
1/2 cup or 1 stick chilled organic cultured butter, cut into 1 inch cubes
1/2 cup maple syrup
2 large eggs
3/4 teaspoon apple cider vinegar

Method:

1. Preheat the oven to 350 degrees. Line a baking sheet with parchment paper and set aside.
2. In the work bowl of a food processor, add the oat flour, potato starch, baking soda, salt and cinnamon and process until combined.
3. Transfer the flour mixture to a large bowl and add the cold butter cubes. With a pastry cutter or fork, work the butter into the flour until the texture of the flour resembles a coarse sand and the butter is about the size of a pea.
4. In a small bowl, whisk the eggs. Whisk in the maple syrup and vinegar. Pour into the flour mixture and mix briefly–just until the dough comes together. Do not over mix.
5. With an ice cream scooper or 1/4 cup measuring cup, scoop the dough onto baking sheet with 2 inches between each scone.
6. Bake for 35-40 minutes or until firm and golden. Cool for 15 minutes, cut and serve.

Note: Store in an airtight container for up to 5 days or freeze for up to 3 months.

Cranberry Vanilla Scones

Yields: 8 scones

Ingredients:

1 1/2 cups organic oat flour
1/2 cup potato starch
1/2 teaspoon baking soda
1/2 teaspoon kosher salt
1/2 cup or 1 stick chilled organic cultured butter, cut into 1 inch cubes
2 large eggs
1 tablespoon vanilla extract
1/2 cup maple syrup
3/4 teaspoon apple cider vinegar
1 cup dried cranberries

Method:

1. Preheat the oven to 350 degrees. Line a baking sheet with parchment paper and set aside.
2. In the work bowl of a food processor, add the oat flour, potato starch, baking soda, salt and cinnamon and process until combined.
3. Transfer the flour mixture to a large bowl and add the cold butter cubes. With a pastry cutter or fork, work the butter into the flour until the texture of the flour resembles a coarse sand and the butter is about the size of a pea.
4. In a small bowl, whisk the eggs and vanilla. Whisk in the maple syrup and vinegar. Pour into the flour mixture and mix briefly–just until the dough comes together. Do not over mix. Add the dried cranberries and gently fold in to combine.
5. With an ice cream scooper or 1/4 cup measuring cup, scoop the dough onto baking sheet with 2 inches between each scone.
6. Bake for 35-40 minutes or until firm and golden. Cool for 15 minutes, cut and serve.

Note: Store in an airtight container for up to 5 days or freeze for up to 3 months.

Brownies

Yield: 1 (8 x 11 inch) pan

Ingredients:

1/2 cup organic cultured butter, cut into cubes
8 ounces dark chocolate chips (Enjoy Life brand - dairy, nut & soy free)
1 teaspoon vanilla extract
3/4 cup maple syrup
1/2 cup oat flour
1 tablespoon coconut flour
1 tablespoon arrowroot powder
1/4 teaspoon sea salt
1/4 teaspoon baking soda
4 large eggs

Method:

1. Preheat the oven to 350 degrees. Lightly grease an 8 x 11 inch baking dish with coconut oil and set aside.
2. In a double boiler bring 1-2 inches of water to a boil. Reduce to a simmer and place a heatproof glass or metal bowl over the top of the saucepan. Add the chocolate chips and butter and slowly melt together, stirring constantly making sure the chocolate does not burn. Mix in the vanilla, turn off heat, set aside and allow to come to room temperature.
3. In the work bowl of the food processor add the maple syrup, oat flour, coconut flour, arrowroot powder, salt and baking soda and blend until well combined. Add the melted chocolate and blend until smooth.
4. With the motor of the food processor running, add the eggs one at a time and blend until fully combined.
5. Pour the batter into the prepared baking dish and bake for 40 minutes, until a toothpick comes out clean when inserted in the center. Allow to cool in the pan for 30 minutes, cut and serve!

Note: Store in an airtight container for up to 5 days or freeze for up to 3 months.

Chocolate Chip Chickpea Cookie Pie

Yields: 1 10-inch pie

Ingredients:

2 14-ounce cans organic chickpeas, drained and rinsed
1 cup organic quick oats
1/4 cup unsweetened applesauce
3 tablespoons coconut oil, melted
2 teaspoons vanilla extract
1/2 teaspoon baking soda
2 teaspoons baking powder
1/2 teaspoon salt
2/3 cup maple syrup
1 cup dark chocolate chips (Enjoy Life brand - dairy, nut & soy free)

Method:

1. Preheat the oven to 350 degrees. Line a 10 inch round cake pan with parchment paper and grease with cooking spray. Set aside.
2. In the work bowl of a food processor, add the chickpeas, oats, applesauce, coconut oil, vanilla, baking soda, baking powder, salt and maple syrup. Process until smooth.
3. With a spatula, mix in chocolate chips and pour the batter into the prepared cake pan.
4. Bake for 40 minutes. Remove from the oven and let stand until cooled, about 15 minutes.
5. With a butter knife, separate the crust of the pie from the sides of the cake pan. Place a large plate on top of the cake pan and quickly flip the pan upside down to remove the pie from cake pan. Place a serving plate on top of the now inverted cookie pie and flip so that the pie is now right side up.
6. Slice and serve.

Pumpkin Loaf

Yield: 1 (8 1/2 x 4 1/2 inch) loaf

Ingredients:

2 large eggs
3/4 cup unsweetened sunflower seed butter
1/2 cup maple syrup
1/2 cup organic pumpkin puree
3 tablespoons coconut oil, softened
2 teaspoons lemon juice
1 teaspoon vanilla extract
1/2 cup arrowroot powder
1 1/2 tablespoons ground cinnamon
2 teaspoons ground nutmeg
2 teaspoons baking powder
1/2 teaspoon lemon zest
1/2 teaspoon ground ginger
1/4 teaspoon sea salt

Method:

1. Preheat the oven to 350 degrees. Lightly grease the loaf pan with coconut oil and set aside.
2. In the work bowl of a food processor, combine the eggs, sunflower seed butter, maple syrup, pumpkin puree, coconut oil, lemon juice and vanilla extract. Blend until smooth, about 1 minute.
3. Add the arrowroot powder, cinnamon, nutmeg, baking powder, lemon zest, ginger and salt. Blend for another minute more until well combined.
4. Pour the batter into the prepared loaf pan. Bake for 1 hour until a toothpick comes out clean when inserted into the middle of the loaf.
5. Remove the loaf from the oven and allow to cool in the pan for about 20 minutes.

So Good Chocolate Chip Cookies

Ingredients:

1 1/2 cups organic oat flour
1/2 cup potato starch, plus a little extra for the work surface
1/2 teaspoon baking soda
1/2 teaspoon kosher salt
1/2 cup or 1 stick chilled unsalted butter, cut into 1 inch cubes
1/2 cup maple syrup
2 large eggs
3/4 teaspoon apple cider vinegar or lemon juice
1/2 cup dark chocolate chips (Enjoy Life brand - dairy, nut & soy free)

Method:

1. Preheat the oven to 350 degrees. Line a baking sheet with parchment paper and set aside.
2. In the work bowl of a food processor, add the oat flour, potato starch, baking soda and salt and process until combined.
3. Add the cold butter cubes to the processor and pulse until the flour resembles a coarse sand and the butter is about the size of a pea.
4. Add the maple syrup, eggs, and vinegar and process just until the dough comes together. Transfer the cookie batter to a bowl and fold in the chocolate chips.
5. With an ice cream scooper or 1/4 cup measuring cup, scoop the dough onto baking sheet with 2 inches between each cookie.
6. Bake for 35-40 minutes or until firm and golden. Cool for 15 minutes, cut and serve.

Notes

Made in the USA
Monee, IL
23 March 2021